Caleb Fleming

The Doctrine of the Eucharist

considered as a distinguishing ritual in the social worship of Christians - with some account of the erroneous and superstitious notions, which have obtained concerning it

Caleb Fleming

The Doctrine of the Eucharist

considered as a distinguishing ritual in the social worship of Christians - with some account of the erroneous and superstitious notions, which have obtained concerning it

ISBN/EAN: 9783337286453

Printed in Europe, USA, Canada, Australia, Japan

Cover: Foto ©Lupo / pixelio.de

More available books at **www.hansebooks.com**

THE DOCTRINE OF THE EUCHARIST,

CONSIDERED

As a diftinguifhing ritual in the focial worfhip of chriftians.

WITH

Some account of the erroneous and fuperftitious notions, which have obtained concerning it.

By CALEB FLEMING.

And upon the firſt day of the week, the diſciples came together to BREAK BREAD.   St. LUKE.

This is not to eat the LORD'S SUPPER.   St. PAUL.

LONDON:

Printed for C. HENDERSON, under the Royal Exchange; and T. BECKET, and P. A. DE HONT, in the Strand. 1763.

A DEDICATION.

TO the serious and rational communicant; and to those pious professors, who see not the doctrine of the Eucharist in a clear and convincing light; are these sheets humbly dedicated: in hopes of giving some fresh aid to the devotions of the former; and of removing prejudice and prepossession from the latter.

As to those *sons of levity or impiety*, who dare ridicule a divine institution; the sneer and laugh will be excited in them, by the very advertisement. Others of more decent character, but who disbelieve a revelation, will be apt to call it *priestcraft*, and an ancient artful church method of deluding the people. Among the devotional, those crowds of *enthusiasts*, who can be persuaded to follow TEACHERS, that are vain enough

DEDICATION.

enough to pretend to new revelations, to viſions, and even to miraculous operations; theſe will be very unlikely to make any uſe of this performance. And when we add the yet more numerous *ſons of ſuperſtition*, it may be aſked, what poſſible motive could induce to this publication concerning the Euchariſt? The anſwer is, "an apparently "great indifference ſhewn the ri- "tual, among profeſſors of a more "rational ſpirit and generous com- "plexion."—

If with theſe open, ingenuous, liberal minds, this attempt ſhould have any good impreſſion; the end will be attained, which is the principal aim,

Of their devoted,

humble ſervant,

Hoxton Square.

C. F.

A plan of the work.

The introduction; which states the evidence of the *New Testament* canon.

Sec. I. The divine original of the Eucharist.

II. The social nature of the ritual, with the sensible symbols requisite to the celebration.

III. The spiritual nature of the Eucharist.

IV. The persons who are properly qualified for the celebration.

V. The obligation to celebrate the Eucharist, perpetual.

VI. The erroneous and superstitious opinions which have obtained concerning the Eucharist.

VII. Observations made on the doctrine.

THE INTRODUCTION;

Which states the evidence of the New Testament canon.

LITTLE advantage could be proposed from explaining the doctrine of the Eucharist, if the authenticity and authority of the *New Testament* writings should be held doubtful. The *evidence* of their certainly being a *divine canon* of faith and manners, to all who will give them a religious attention, may be thus collected.—
" The *fact* of there having been a man, who
" appeared in *Judea* between seventeen and
" eighteen

" eighteen hundred years ago, named JESUS
" CHRIST, *a prophet mighty in deed and*
" *word before God, and all the people!* is as
" inconteſtable, as that there ever was ſuch
" a man as *Homer, Socrates, Plato, Virgil,*
" *Julius Cæſar,* or even *Mahomet*; not one
" of all which have equal evidence of hav-
" ing exiſted with any remarkable or diſtin-
" guiſhed character."

That the perſonal miniſtrations of Jeſus were confined to *Judea,* the land of his nativity, and to a people to whom he had been deſcribed in prophecy, as a *ſaviour* and *redeemer*; but whoſe inſtructions and miniſtrations were to become *a light to enlighten the Gentile or Pagan world, as well as be the glory of his people Iſrael.*—That accordingly, he did ordain a number of diſciples, who conſtantly attended his miniſtry, to be the publiſhers of his doctrine throughout the world, after he had riſen from the dead, and was aſcended into heaven, in the ſight of thoſe choſen witneſſes.—A farther demonſtration of his being exalted to the right hand
of

of power, was given by *extraordinary gifts*, which were conferred on them, in accomplishment of a promise which he had made them before his death; and of which miraculous heavenly vouchsafement, great numbers of Jews were witnesses, which came from very distant countries.

The notoriety of this fact became universal, by the apostles (when so qualified) going into all parts of the world to publish the gospel; of whose labours, oppositions, difficulties and successes, a natural and genuine account is given in an history of their acts, and in epistles written by their own hands, and sent to the churches which they at first planted. In which writings there are no marks of artifice, fraud, or policy; none of sinister aim, or of sordid intention: but all the evidences of an heavenly disposition and a divine spirit, in each and every of their doctrinal instructions, altogether suitable to the dignified character and divine appointments of their master.

The *New Testament* scriptures have no resemblance, no similitude of the writings of uninspired men: and they also are harmonious in their spiritual, heavenly, and moral representations.

The age of apostles was properly denominated, the *manifestation* or *dispensation of the spirit:* they themselves being to the world the living oracles of God, as Jesus Christ their master had been, during his ministration, to the people of *Judea*. And because they were able ministers of the *New Testament*, the ministration of the spirit by them, must have far exceeded in glory all former dispensations.

But because *this light of the knowledge of God in the face of Jesus Christ, was a treasure deposited in earthen vessels*; apostles, like other men, being subject to mortality; it became absolutely needful that a *written record* should be made of the life and teachings of Jesus, the canon of faith and practice to all succeeding ages of christians; since the
gifts

gifts of the spirit must cease, when ever that testimony was finished which they were designed to give to the mission of apostles.

That the *New Testament* written canon must have been compleated during the age of apostles, is also evident; because none but they were capable infallible judges, which could authenticate the record. Hence it was, that St. PAUL, who had not been a disciple and personal attendant on Jesus, or a witness of his resurrection and ascension, was favoured with *visions* and *revelations*, and conversed with the exalted Jesus; and likewise received from him *gifts of the spirit* equal to those of the other apostles; which rendered him capable of revising and establishing the credit of St. *Mark*'s gospel.

Here an observation, made by our ecclesiastical historian, will be pertinent. " A
" short canon of scripture is most eligible.
" Religion is the concern of all men. A
" few short histories and epistles are better
" fitted for general use, than numerous and
" prolix

"prolix writings. Befides, if any writings are to be received as the rule of faith and manners, it is of the utmoft importance that they be juftly entitled to that diftinction; otherwife men may be led into errors of very bad confequence. If any books pretend to deliver the doctrine of infallible and divinely infpired teachers, fuch as Jefus Chrift and his apoftles are efteemed by chriftians, great care fhould be taken to be well fatisfied that their accounts are authentic, and that they are the genuine writings of the men, whofe names they bear*." *N. B.* The public is greatly indebted to the labours of this author, for laying before the eye of his reader a feries of teftimony to the canon of the *New Teftament*, which reaches down even to the twelfth century, in that work of his, entitled, *The Credibility of the Gofpel Hiftory.*

We are now able to give a very fatisfactory folution to that fceptical queftion, *viz.* " How can we, at this diftance of time and

---

* See Dr. LARDNER's fupplement, vol. I. ch. ii. p. 27.

" place,

" place, be assured what is, and what is not
" divine canon, when there are no *auto-*
" *graphs*, either of epistles by apostles, or of
" gospels by their authors?"

Assured we are, that those writings which we have, cannot materially differ from their originals; because of the jealous eye christians could not but have upon one another, on account of different opinion and mode of profession. The several languages into which they were translated, (the gospel doctrine having been previously propagated by apostles, in different nations) would render it impracticable or impossible for men to have made any alteration, of importance, in the divine canon. We therefore have all the moral certainty that can possibly attend the conveyance of an heavenly instruction. Nay, besides this, the complexion of these writings will suit no other age of the world, so well as they do that in which they are said to have been written.*

* See Dr. LARDNER's *first part of the credibility*, &c. where the facts occasionally mentioned by evangelists are confirmed by ancient cotemporary authors.

Moreover,

Moreover, as to the intrinſic or internal evidence, we, at this day are as capable of examining, judging and determining, as men ever were in any one age of the chriſtian profeſſion: of the moral, ſpiritual and heavenly nature, and tendency of the canon, every man is able to make an infallible judgment, by conforming his temper and life to its guidance and direction.—

They do therefore manifeſtly miſtake in judging of this canon, who will have the *New Teſtament* writings to be no other than a *ſecondary rule*, and the ſpirit, or light within them to be the *primary* one; whereas the reaſon, or ſpirit of a man, is more properly and truly the judge of the one written cannon, or rule, than the primary rule itſelf. But the miſtake ſeems to be owing to a wrong interpretation of the apoſtle, as if in an oppoſition of the *letter* to the *ſpirit*, he could be underſtood of the letter of the written goſpel, oppoſed to the manifeſtation of the ſpirit; which is not to illuſtrate, but to confound his meaning. The *letter* which he oppoſes to the *ſpirit*, could

could be no other than the Mosaic system; which, he largely shews, had nothing in it that would compare with the spiritual manifestation of truth and grace, made by the gospel. *Moreover*, those very people, who would have the written gospel to be no better than a *secondary* rule, and who give preference to the light within, or to the teachings of the spirit, do professedly borrow all their notions of the spirit from the written word*; which reflects upon them an apparent absurdity.—They seem not to have attended to the difference of circumstance in which christians were, when under the dispensation of the spirit, before the written canon had existence, and whilst the spirit was the primary and only rule; and the condition of christians, when the dispensation of the spirit had wholly ceased with the finished ages of the apostles, and when the written gospel was

---

* We shall be willing to admit it, as a positive certain maxim, that whatsoever any do, pretending to the spirit, which is contrary to the scriptures, be accounted and reckoned a delusion of the devil. *Barclay*'s apology, p. 86.

become the only divine rule to the whole church of Chriſt.

Others, with deſign to invalidate the *rule*, have ſaid, "that Jeſus never gave any expreſs orders that men ſhould write an hiſtory of his life."

This is readily acknowledged: nor was there the leaſt occaſion for his giving ſuch direction. He well knew that thoſe his diſciples, whom he had ordained to publiſh his goſpel to the world, ſhould receive *the promiſe of the father*, and have extraordinary divine illuminations. He alſo knew that the deſign of his doctrine and miſſion, was to be of univerſal and perpetual uſe and benefit to mankind; and that therefore they could not fail of making a written-record, ere the diſpenſation of the ſpirit ſhould finiſh. He infallibly knew that ſuch a divine teſtimony, which had been given of him, muſt be tranſmitted to the laſt age of mankind.

The objection seems also to be unnatural and capricious; for men are not wont to inquire of *biographers* (who have, with great attention and labour, composed and published the lives of great men) whether their *heroes* had desired it at their hands? what will fully justify the historian, and also entitle him to the thanks of the public, is, if his subject was every way worthy a record; if it promised universal pleasure and profit, in the perusal; for then, verily we ascribe great merit, and do such *biographers* deserved honour. On this principle it is, we reverence the names of the sacred writers, who composed the canon of the *New Testament*.

But the objection entirely vanishes, when we read what the beloved disciple says in his own defence, as an historian,—" and many
" other signs truly did Jesus in the presence
" of his disciples, which are not written in
" this book. But these *are written*, that ye
" might believe that Jesus is the Christ, the
" son of the living God, and that believing
" ye

" ye might have life through his name."—
And *again*, "this is the difciple which tefti-
" fieth of thefe things, and *wrote thefe things*;
" and we know that his teftimony is true.
" And there are alfo many other things
" which Jefus did, the which, if they fhould
" *be written*, every one, I fuppofe, that even
" the world itfelf would not contain or re-
" ceive the books that fhould be written."
That is, they would be much too bulky
and voluminous for common ufe; and would
not fo officioufly anfwer the end of a divine
canon. Compare *John* xx. 30, 31. *ch.* xxi,
24, 25. But who can once call in queftion
the propriety of fuch a record, that confi-
ders the nature and tendency of it?

SECTION I.

The divine original of the Eucharist.

WHEN we write or speak concerning a religious observance, or a divine institution, we ought to be well satisfied of its heavenly *original*. And when it concerns christian practice, it must have place in that canon esteemed sacred by the common consent of christians, which canon is called, the *New Testament writings*; containing the only genuine life of Christ, his heavenly and divine teachings, as recorded by apostles and evangelists.

St. *Matthew, Mark, Luke* and *Paul*, have each of them assured us, that the *Eucharist*
was

was inſtituted by Jeſus Chriſt himſelf, the very evening before his ſufferings, *Matth.* xxvi. 26.—*Mark* xiv. 22.—*Luke* xxii. 19. 1 *Cor.* ii. 23.—And we may reaſonably account for the ſilence of St. *John,* who only wrote a ſupplemental goſpel*. Yet, even this evangeliſt has given us thoſe diſcourſes of our Lord's, delivered immediately before his ſufferings, which enable us to enter more fully into the meaning or ſpirit of the memorial inſtitution. And beſides thoſe diſcourſes, it ſhould ſeem that he foreſaw the ſuperſtitious and extravagant notions which men would entertain of the Euchariſt; and therefore was led to inſert another diſcourſe, which our Lord delivered concerning his *doctrine,* being, that his fleſh which men ſhould eat, and that his blood which men ſhould drink, the internal principle of immortality. St. *John*'s ſilence about the Euchariſt is thus well accounted for; and we have reaſon to conclude, he ſaw that the celebration of it did, in his day, univerſally obtain

---

* Conſult Dr. LARDNER's ſupplement, vol. I. ch. ix. ſec. x.

among chriſtians. The *authority* on which the ritual ſupports, is thus indiſputable.

That it could have no other original than what the above writers report it to have had, is alſo evident from its very obvious intention; which is, to commemorate the fact of the man Chriſt Jeſus dying as a malefactor, by public conſent of his own nation; notwithſtanding he had been approved of God among them, by ſigns, wonders, and divers miracles, which were wrought by him.— That a *thankſgiving* memorial ſhould be appointed, is contrary to all the uſages and cuſtoms of mankind; who, to expreſs their deteſtation and abhorrence of the cruel treatment of great and good men, would have inſtituted ſome monument of indignation, of ſhame and ſorrow, rather than of congratulation, thankfulneſs and joy. There is therefore in the very complexion of the ritual, a ſpirit and intention diſcoverable, which is the reverſe of all civil and political appointments. And, in fact, ſo ſtood the celebration of the Euchariſt among the firſt chriſtians;

tians; it was an open devout acknowledgment, that the *stigma* of reproach, which had been fixed on their divine master, by his crucifixion, was esteemed by them, matter of their boasting and glory. They thus recognized his distinguished merit, and superior excellence! and hereby the reputation and credit of their religion was highly recommended to the world. So far from being ashamed of his cross, they considered it as a vain, fruitless attempt of his ungrateful malicious enemies, to suppress his heavenly doctrine, and to blemish his divine character in the eyes of the nations.

A more direct and full confutation of envy and detraction, surely could not have been given. Divine wisdom thus displays itself in the open face of the institution; without which, the christian profession would have been exposed to public scorn and universal contempt. For had there been any possible impeachment of crime in his character, or any defect shewn in his divine claims, whom they had crucified as an impostor, the profession

feſſion would have been ſtifled in its infancy, and all his diſciples covered with ſhame and infamy. But, on the contrary, what could be a more convincing proof of the confidence which they had in him, than their open celebration of his death, by a thankful and joyful memorial?

On this *ratio* ſtood the divine original of the Euchariſt, in the obſervance of firſt chriſtians, when the ſcandal of the croſs was recent and popular; and unleſs a man is determined to ſhut his eyes againſt evidence, he is conſtrained to own the inſtitution to be reaſonable, and divinely well adapted to thoſe moſt uſeful ends it was deſigned to anſwer. Not like a merely poſitive and arbitrary appointment; but, with all other moral and divine inſtruction, it ſpeaks the language of inconteſtable facts, and ſupports on the manifeſt law of relation, as will be more clearly ſeen by and by.

The ſenſe now given of the *divine original* of the Euchariſt, will be abundantly confirmed *by the epiſtles,* and by St. *Luke's hiſtory of the acts of the apostles.* In the epistles, we frequently find St. *Paul* speaking of *the cross of Christ,* as matter and occasion of his greatest glorying. He looked upon it as a divine scheme, "which had destroyed the wisdom of the wise; and brought to nothing the understanding of the prudent.—Which was to the *Jews* a stumbling block, and to the *Greeks* foolishness." And yet, to the christian, it was no other than the power of God, and the wisdom of God. In what sense *the cross of Christ* may be understood, *the power of God and the wisdom of God,* will be of easy conception, when it is considered how Christ becomes a *Saviour* and *Redeemer,* viz. by delivering men from the evil of this present world; and by inspiring them with spiritual and heavenly affections. Which redemption could not have been accomplished by him, had he not actually submitted to the deepest possible abasement, and taken into the compass of his trial the whole energy of temptation: for by this means only could he become the author and finisher of our faith, as he thereby shewed the practicability, as well as possibility of overcoming all the efforts of evil.

evil. On the cross he exemplified a contempt of the world, by a superiority of mind to all sensible impressions, however shameful or painful. And in the greatness of his behaviour, throughout the scenery of his humiliation *, he discovered a meetness for that majesty and dominion, to which the one God did exalt him, in reward of his obedience to the death.

The divine original of the Eucharist will be yet further obvious, from the design of that very death, which it commemorates, *viz.* God's *reconciling the world to himself* by that event. For verily, mankind do receive from thence the most important and interesting instruction, in all moral and divine truths; *e. g.* they are shewn how very merciful a being he is, that could pardon the murderers of that his well-beloved son, *who made it his meat to do the will of his father, and to finish his work:* who did not dispute the most painful endurance; cordially saying, *not my will, but*

* See this illustrated with great address, in Dr. Lardner's 2d vol. of sermons.

thine be done: and to whom the Deity had given miraculous teftimony of his approbation. When therefore we are informed of great numbers of Chrift's murderers obtaining pardon, and encouraged to hope for eternal life! the reprefentation is fuited to reconcile the mind of a penitent finner, and reftore him to peace. Thus God is faid *to be reconciling the world unto himfelf, not imputing to* penitent *men their trefpaffes.*

Another view of the *reconciliation* is, that of mankind being no longer allowed to form a judgment of the approbation or difapprobation of God towards them, becaufe of external circumftance or condition: fince the moft beloved and honoured of God, *was defpifed and rejected of men. A man of forrows, and acquainted with griefs.* Hence the moft abject condition, and painful endurance of man is altogether confiftent with virtuous character, and with his enjoyment of the divine favour. Whilft the moft profperous external circumftance, and elevated rank of civil condition, may be the allotment of the

moft

moſt unworthy of mortals. Thus the ſufferings and death of Jeſus have, in them, an apt tendency *to reconcile men to God*, as they correct and cure the prejudices which ariſe from ſenſible impreſſions that are made upon us.

A *third* reconciling view of Chriſt's death may be taken from its *rewardableneſs*. Who, *for the joy ſet before him, did endure the croſs and deſpiſe the ſhame*. And, in virtue of his *obedience to the death, he had a name* GIVEN *him above every name* *; even that of the reſurrection

* The Rev. Mr. THOMAS EMLYN ſays, "a gift
" of no *new* authority ſeems to be a gift of nothing. Is
" Chriſt rewarded with nothing, or with no addition
" of glory? muſt he hold that by gift, which he held
" by a better tenure before?"—See his works, 4th edit. vol. I. p. 247.

And to the ſame purpoſe we have the concurring judgment of the Rev. Mr. JAMES PIERCE.—" It has
" been the common opinion of ancient chriſtians, as
" well as it is of the generality of the modern writers
" upon the ſcriptures, that in many, or at leaſt in ſome
" of the appearances of the angels recorded in the *Old*
" *Teſtament*, the λογ⊙, the ſon himſelf was one of the
" number.—But it may be queſtioned whether that
" opinion hath any ſolid foundation. I know not of
" any

surrection and the life; the Lord of the dead and of the living; and the final judge. It is in him that we have the earneſt of the inheritance, to whom God has given the keys of hades and of death. A demonſtration of his having ſuch an inveſtiture of ſovereignty, is ſeen in the ſubſequent miraculous gifts beſtowed on apoſtles, who were to preach or publiſh his goſpel throughout the world.

From the reward of his obedience, the ſincere chriſtian is encouraged to look and wait "for his Lord's coming to receive him
" to himſelf, to be with him where he is, to
" behold the glory which the father hath

" any place of ſcripture where it is expreſsly aſſerted:
" and the arguments brought to prove it, are ſo very
" ſlight, that it ſeems at beſt to be a mere conjecture.
" There is, at leaſt nothing in this epiſtle to favour it,
" but the contrary." See his note *(d)* on *Heb.* i. 2. with which may be compared his note *(c)* on ch. iii. 36.

With theſe teſtimonies agree the Rev. Mr. MOSES LOWMAN's three *tracts on the Shechinah and Logos*; *and the letter writ in the year* 1730, all of which do virtually maintain this concluſion, *viz.* " that the ex-
" altation of Chriſt muſt have been in *reward* of his
" obedience to the death; inaſmuch as we have no rea-
" ſon to ſuppoſe any manifeſtation of him antecedent *to*
" *his being born of a woman, and made under the law.*"

" given

"given him." And an apostle thus reasoneth, *if we are reconciled to God by the death of his son, how much more shall we be saved by his life?*—Another says, *baptism does now save us by the resurrection of Jesus Christ, who is gone into heaven.* The *death of Christ* verily, has all its efficacy and energy derived from its consequences. Separate from these his death has in it no one useful, or instructive meaning. In the abstract idea of it there could be no reason of thanksgiving or joy. But when we once know that death could not hold him, as a trophy or prisoner; and that it was *impossible for this God's holy one to see corruption*, because he could not die as a criminal; we discern how this circumstance determines him to be the son of God and Saviour of the world. From the rewardableness of his death, we then derive benefits, in size and number, considerable enough to excite and animate all our gratitude and praise; forasmuch as we can also rely on a spiritual and moral union with *him* who is our powerful head. Under whose administration, we are even assured of an happy immortality, St. *Peter* having given us this very

very engaging representation of those benefits, when he says, *blessed be the God and father of our Lord Jesus Christ, which according to his abundant mercy hath begotten us again unto a lively hope, by the resurrection of Jesus Christ from the dead, to an inheritance incorruptible, and undefiled, aud that fadeth not away, reserved in the heavens for us.*

Objection. Should it not now be asked, why has God taken this method of conferring his favours on mankind? Is there not something in it too obscure and mysterious for ordinary conception?

Ans. So far from it, that of all other known methods of revealing his truth and grace, this seems to be the most familiar and engaging in its instruction; forasmuch as it most naturally suits with the condition of man, both as subjected to death, and also as interested in a resurrection from the dead. Whatever were the informations otherways given about these things, there never had been any instructor, in whom, as a common head, power was invested to preside *as Lord over*

over both the dead and living. Whereas, in Jesus, the dominion of death is made void; and immortal life is brought to light by his instructions. We are thus, by him, enabled to view death with composure, and the future state with joyful hope. Our ideas have a clearness and precision in them; and we are not left to the random guesses of an unguided imagination, nor to the visions of poets, or dreams of philosophers. The veil, that terrified the mind by its gloom, is quite thrown aside *again*, the making manifest by the death of Christ, and its consequences, is in perfect harmony with nature, and the universal voice of providence. For, should we inquire what are the advantages we receive relative to this system? or what the method of their conveyance? they will be found essential to our present subsistence, and to be conveyed, ordinarily, thro' the hands of our fellow men, *i. e.* some way by their instrumentality. We certainly owe the various and numerous accommodations of life and being, to their ministrations and mediations. This allowed to be the case, no measure could be more worthy of God, than that of appointing

pointing *him* to be the captain of our salvation, who partook of flesh and blood; and was in all things made like to his brethren : and who verily was perfected through sufferings. *A man tempted as we are, touched with the feeling of our infirmities,* can best sympathize with us, and best succour us under the whole of our trial.

An objection that could arise to this divine scheme, would equally disrelish any other known medium of manifestation. But, of a truth, it was very unlikely, that PROPHECY should mark out the Messiah from the first age of the world; and yet, that there should not be some great meaning, some universal advantage arise from his mission and appointments, whenever he should make his appearance.—Thus it is presumed, the *divine origin* of the memorial of Christ's death is shewn with evidence.

§. II.

§. II. *The social nature of the ritual, with the sensible symbols requisite to the celebration.*

That the Eucharist is to be celebrated *socially*, and with the visible sensible symbols of material bread and material wine, which are for the participation of each and every communicant, might be argued from those accounts the sacred writers have given of the institution. Not any thing less than a violence offered to the text, can give any other sense of the ritual. Our blessed Lord, after the pascal feast, " took bread, and gave
" thanks, he took the cup also and gave
" thanks, and bade them all drink of it.—
" He said of the bread, take, eat, *this is my*
" *body:* to distinguish it from the passover-
" lamb, which had a quite different object.
" And of the cup, he says, *this is the New*
" *Testament in my bloud,* which is as widely
" different from the intention of the pascal
" cup of thanksgiving. So St. *Paul* says,
" the cup of blessing which we bless, is it
" not the communion of the bloud of
" Christ? and the bread which we break,
" is

" is it not the communion of the body of
" Chrift?"—That fort of *bleffing* and *praifing* God, ufed over the bread and over the cup, did intend the feparating of them from common to a religious ufe: *i. e.* they are not to be taken to fatisfy hunger or thirft; but are to be the fymbols of *his* body broken, and *his* bloud fhed, who inftituted the memorial. And they are to be eaten and drank in *fociety*, to denote the fpiritual communion which chriftians have with one another, and alfo their union with the one Lord.

But the tranfaction being focial, is alfo manifeft from the practice of the firft chriftians; of whom St. *Luke* fays, that *on the firft day of the week the difciples came together to break bread.* Acts xx. 7. compare *ch.* ii. 46. And with him agrees St. *Paul*, who when he wrote to the Corinthians about the year 56, obferves, *when they came together into one place, they could not eat the Lord's fupper*; for this reafon, *viz.* they divided into feparate companies, even in the place of public worfhip, and every one eat his own fupper: one was hungry,

gry, and another was drunken.—They forgot that their own houses were most proper, in which to eat their common meals, and not the church of God; and that they altogether thus perverted the spiritual nature and intention of the memorial rite: for, *they being many, were one bread and one body; as they were all to partake alike of that one bread.*

We have a pagan testimony much to our purpose, *viz.* that of PLINY, who thus writes of the christians, in his letter to TRAJAN: " the whole of their guilt, is, they
" meet on a certain stated day, before it is
" light, and address themselves in the form
" of a prayer to Christ, as to some God,*
" binding themselves by a solemn oath, not
" for the purposes of any wicked design, but
" never to commit any fraud, theft, or adul-
" tery, never to falsify their word, nor deny
" a trust when called upon to deliver it up;

---

*. In the Oxford edit. of 1667, this is the phrase, *carmenq; christo, quasi deo, dicere secum invicem*, which I should render, " each of them sung an hymn to " Christ, as to a God." *q. d.* much resembling the way we have of doing honour to one of our deities.

" after

"after which it was their cuſtom to ſeparate, and then re-aſſemble, to eat in common an harmleſs meal."*

An early honourable teſtimony given by the *Roman* governor of a province to an emperor, who flouriſhed about the year of Chriſt, one hundred. The harmleſs meal which he reports the Chriſtians to have eaten in common, was undoubtedly the *Eucharist*. It is mentioned as a part of their ſocial and religious obſervance, a ſtated thing among them. And he alſo obſerves, the pure unblemiſhed morality of their profeſſion; "they bind themſelves by a ſolemn oath, not to do any thing that would reproach their holy religion. Herein following that apoſtolic rule, *walk ye worthy of that vocation wherewith ye are called.*"

Another ſucceeding teſtimony I would produce, is, from *Juſtin Martyr,* in his firſt apology preſented to the emperor and ſenate of *Rome,* about the year of Chriſt one hun-

* PLINY's letters, book x. letter 97, MELMOTH's tranſlation.

dred and forty, giving an account of the chriftian worfhip; who expreffes himfelf after this manner. "And after prayer, there
"is brought to him who prefides over the
"brethren, bread (or a loaf) and a cup of
"water and wine, which he takes, and
"then gives praife and glory to the father of
"the univerfe, in the name of the fon and
"of the holy fpirit. And after finifhing the
"prayer and thankfgiving, all the people pre-
"fent give their affent, faying, *amen*. Then
"they who with us are called *deacons*, give
"the bread, and the wine and water to every
"one prefent, and fend to fuch as are ab-
"fent. This food is called by us the *Eu-*
"*charift*, of which no one may partake but
"he who believes the things taught by us,
"and has been wafhed in the laver for the
"remiffion of fins and regeneration, and to
"live as Chrift hath commanded. For we
"do not take this as common bread, or
"common drink. For the apoftles in
"their memoirs, which are called *gofpels*,
"have delivered it to us, that Chrift directed
"it fo to be done: and that when he had
"taken

"taken bread and given thanks, he said, "*do this in remembrance of me, this is my* "*body.* And in like manner, that having "taken the cup, and given thanks, he said, "*this is my bloud,* and gave it to them only." p. 82, 83. edit. *Bened.*

An apology presented to the emperor *Antoninus Pius*, and the senate, is a testimony of great notoriety and high credit, and in full proof of the social nature of the ritual, and of the use of sensible material symbols in the celebration. At the same time, their *sending the elements to such christians who were absent*, must, confessedly be an instance of departure from the letter of the divine canon, and of apostolic practice.

It would not be wide of the point, to mention the farther testimony of TATIAN, a disciple of *Justin Martyr*, who represents the Lord's supper and the design of it, as a memorial in this manner; "and "having taken bread (or a loaf) and then a "cup of wine, and having said that they

were

" were his body and bloud, he commanded
" them to eat and drink; for it was (or they
" were) a memorial of his future suffering and
" death.*" This testimony was about the year
one hundred and seventy. And though it does
not explicitly report the practice of christians,
yet it gives us reason to suppose that the institution was then so understood, and so celebrated, *viz.* by a social religious eating of material bread, and drinking of material wine in memory of Christ's sufferings and death.

We can add, that *Justin Martyr, Tertullian, Cyprian* and *Origen*, have given very express accounts of the *Lord's Supper*; not only as to the time of receiving, and persons who did receive, but also as to the manner of celebration.† Indeed all good writers on ecclesiastical antiquities do agree, in representing the Eucharist, as an essential, distinguishing ritual, celebrated socially among christians.

* See Dr. LARDNER's Credib. P. II. vol. III. B. I. ch. xxxvi. p. 148.
† See Lord KING's enquiry into the constitution, &c. of primitive church, part II. ch. vi.

The social nature of the Eucharist, or the use of sensible symbols in the celebration, might be further argued, from the various alterations made by christians in their observances; such as, "giving it to infants, car"rying the Eucharist home with them to "their own houses, to receive as they had "occasion. The *Eulogiae*, or sending it to "different churches, in token of joint-com"munion;—the changing of the table po"sture to standing in the third century, which "continued to the eleventh, and then to "kneeling;" every of these alterations infer an original social institution. See Dr. WHITBY's *prot. recon.* p. 291, 294.*

---

* It is here observable, that our modern *sectaries*, who implicitly follow their leaders, are fond of mimicking an early custom which the christians had, " of " making entertainments for strangers, or for christian " travellers upon the church's stock." Which laudable custom Dr. LIGHEFOOT thinks was derived from the Jews, viz. the *agapae*, or *feasts of charity*, mentioned *Jude* ver. 12. But what resemblance have the modern *love feasts* ?—See LIGHTFOOT's works, vol. II. p. 775.

§. III,

§. III. *The spiritual nature of the Eucharist.*

There are some who have understood the death of Christ as a *sacrifice*; and the Eucharist as a *feast* upon that sacrifice. And it must be confessed, that there are a number of texts in the *New Testament* that have spoken of him as a propitiation and sacrifice; nay, once he is said to be *our passover sacrificed for us*, 1 Cor. v. 7. But to understand the sacrifical terms, so applied in a literal sense, would be to strain allusions into original facts; and to throw much confusion on the human mind. Such figurative representation was natural and familiar to the eyes of a Jewish convert, who had strong prejudices in favour of the Mosaic ritual: and yet the *Old Testament doctrine of sacrifice* will be found to speak of it, either as the symbol of *penitence*, or of *gratitude*, in the person who presented the victim. But in the death of Christ, so far from penitence being expressed by them who devoted him, he was considered by them as an execrable criminal! they did not therefore express penitence by his death,

death, but ignorance, pride, envy and malice.

Gratitude was as remote from them as penitence; they did not thereby acknowledge obligation for benefits received; but, on the contrary, the moſt flagrant diſingenuity, and the vileſt ingratitude was ſhewn to him, by whom God had healed all the maladies of their people, and given deliverance and ſalvation throughout *Judea*, to their wretched and miſerable! In no one literal and true ſenſe could the death of Jeſus be underſtood, as a *ſacrifice*; when the ſpilling of his bloud was an act of impiety, the moſt horrid that ever could be committed by any people or nation.* It could not then be an expedient to propitiate deity; ſince the inſult and outrage was committed againſt his well-beloved ſon, who had every poſſible atteſtation of divine character and miſſion.

And yet there ſeems to have been an ancient uſe of ſacrifice, to which the death of

* See Pierce's note *(d)* on *Heb.* v. 5, 6.

Chriſt

Chrift may be compared, or to which it may have a very inftructive allufion; and that is, the method of *covenanting* in the patriarchal age. For, upon a divine promife being made by the oracle, on the part of God, with fome condition to be performed on the part of man; the celeftial fire did, in confirmation, confume the facrifice; and thus became a ratifying feal of the covenant, *Gen.* xv. 17. In fuch allufive fenfe, the death of Chrift may have the idea of a facrifice; efpecially when we confider God's raifing him from the dead, and taking him up into heaven, in confirmation of the promife of eternal life, under his adminiftration, and which agrees with the exprefs doctrine of the Eucharift,—*the new teftament in my bloud*. And with St. *Peter*'s report, when he fays,—*who raifed him up from the dead, and gave him glory, that our faith and hope might be in God.* 1 Pet. i. 21.

As to that declaration, *for even Chrift our paffover is facrificed for us*, we may well admit his death to be fitly imaged by an allufion sion to the bloud of the pascal lamb; forasmuch as that bloud sprinkled on the doors of the Israelites, was their security from the destroying angel; whose commission was, at one instant of time, in the dead of the night, to cut off the *first-born* of *Egypt*, both of man and beast. As therefore the bloud of the pascal lamb, was the symbol of safety to the Israelites, so the bloud of Christ is made to us, the symbol of safety from the power of death; for through death he has destroyed him who had the power of death, that is, the devil; or an accusing conscience.* Heb. ii. 14. compared with 1 Cor. xv. 56. *the sting of death is sin.*—But the *bloud of Christ, offered without spot to God, purgeth the conscience from dead works to serve the living God,* Heb. ix. 14. His death demonstrates and convinces of the evil of sin, the malignity of worldliness; and so it purgeth the conscience from whatever would

* Conformable to which sense, *Chrysostom, Theodoret,* and *Theophylact* observe, upon 1 *Cor.* vii. 5. "That it is not satan tempting, but our lusts."—See Dr. Whitby's *Protestant Reconciler*, p. 124, edit. of 1683.

be destructive and deadly. Thus has Christ, by dying, destroyed him that had the power of death, an evil accusing conscience; and by this effect on the human mind, he has abolished death, or made void its dominion. In this allusive sense, Christ is intelligibly said to be, *our passover sacrificed for us*.

A sense in which he is also said to have been *delivered for our offences, to be made sin for us*; and who, as *concerning sin*, περι αμαρτιας, *condemned sin in the flesh*, i. e. in the world, *Rom*. viii. 3. We learn the deadly evil of sin in the death of Christ; we perceive how vicious passions do blind the eye, and harden the heart, and render men capable of any degree of impiety: and upon this conviction wrought in us, we recover to reason and rectitude, and rise to life and immortality.

The death of Christ is often represented as *propitiatory*. And so truly it is, as it reconciles men to truth and God. Christ died to this end; but not to propitiate deity, or render him more merciful in his nature and
disposition

disposition towards man. "God so loved the world, as to give his only begotten son, that whosoever believes in him should not perish, but have eternal life. And Christ also gave himself for us, that he might redeem us from all iniquity, and purify unto himself a peculiar people, zealous of good works." There is no manner of change made in deity by the death of Christ; *but it was according to the will of God, even our father, that he gave himself for our sins, by delivering us from the evil of this present world,* Gal. i. 4. So that, *delivering himself for our sins,* ὑπερ των ἁμαρτιων ἡμων, was, delivering himself for our conviction of the evil of them, and for our deliverance from them. And this was "according to the will of God, and our father, *who would have all men be saved, and come to the knowledge of the truth.*"

The want of seeing the immutable unmerited grace and love of God, as revealed in the gospel, or else the strange desire of finding *mystery* in the death of Christ, has occasioned great confusion and absurdity in men's men's conceptions. And not a few are found refembling the infidel Jews, whofe defires and hopes were confined to the prefent fcenes of fenfible fruition. They want nothing fpiritual, nor to have any concerns in a future ftate of exiftence. No wonder thefe diflike the divinely pure moral of the *New Teftament* fyftem; or that they imagine the fpirit of the gofpel much too refined and heavenly for their tafte and relifh. But, upon a fuppofition of our being defigned for a future exiftence, and that a ftate of recompence muft fucceed this probation; there is no fcheme of inftruction could be more accommodated to both the prefent and future condition of man, than that of the gofpel: for every fober, thoughtful mind muft acknowledge, that all its doctrines, precepts, principles and promifes do fupport on reafon, nature, truth, the law of relation, or the will of God.

This might be confirmed, by obferving, that every *falutary* influence or effect, faid to refult from the death of Chrift, is always expreffive expreſſive of what is ſpiritual and moral. Among numerous paſſages, let the following be conſulted, *Acts* iii. 20. *Rom.* xiv. 8, 9. *Gal.* i. 4. *Tit.* ii. 11, 12. In no one reſpect can the death of Chriſt be the means of ſalvation to any man, further than it promotes his ſpirituality, purity, or morality. Thus only can we conſider the bloud of Chriſt to be propitiatory, as it reconciles us to God.

In a right celebration of the Euchariſt, we expreſs our gratitude and praiſe to the God and father of our Lord Jeſus Chriſt, for the manifeſtation of his truth, and grace made by him: we avow a ſubjection to the ſceptre of this one Lord, by a conformity of temper and life to all his laws, and to the ſpirit of his example; and we renew and re-invigorate our reſolutions to be acquieſcent and reſigned to every divine allotment: we profeſs to live in charity with all mankind, and to have a brotherly affection for all chriſtians: and we alſo declare ourſelves the expectants of our Lord's coming to us, *as a Saviour who will change our vile bodies, and faſhion them like to his glorified body, by that ef-*
fectual

fectual energy, whereby he is even able to subdue all things unto himself. Such is the spiritual and moral nature of the Eucharist, in its original and divine intention.

§. IV. *The persons who are properly qualified for the celebration.*

Every person may be qualified for celebrating the Eucharist, who has the sacred volume of the *New Testament* in his hand, can consult that divine record, and form a judgment of its instruction.—The properly and duly qualified, are such only who do reverence those sacred writings, and religiously attend to them as a divine rule of life, and as the law of the final judgment: conscientiously conforming to all their instruction, and solicitous to improve and establish in those principles of piety and virtue which they inculcate. Moreover, because these scriptures represent it to be the duty of the christian *to examine himself, and so eat of that bread and drink of that cup,* 1 Cor. xi. 28. he will carefully inquire into the nature, design, and end of the Eucharistical celebration, in order that he may *discern the Lord's body**, i. e. he must distinguish it from all other

---

* This, at once, cuts off all priestly pretension: and disallows of any authority in churches to make bye laws, or exclusive terms of christian communion. "A "christian church has its terms and laws settled by "Christ; it is his church, and the table is the *Lord's* "*table*, and the ministers are Christ's ministers: and "it is the highest usurpation in us to make inclosures, "when he has left it open; and to turn out members, "or pastors from their office, if they walk and act ac- "cording to their christian station: and men need be "sure, that the denying their *unscriptural tests* and '*Shibboleths* is such a crime as will justify their pro- "ceedings." See the Rev. Mr. THOMAS EMLYN's *tracts*, vol. I. p. 70. 4th edit.

CHILLINGWORTH says, "take away this perse- ",cuting, burning, cursing, damning of men for not "subscribing to the *words of men*, as the words of God. "Require of christians only to believe Christ, and *to* "*call no man master*, but him only; let those leave "claiming infallibility, who have no title to it; and "let them who in words disclaim it, disclaim it also "in their actions; in a word, take away tyranny, "which is the devil's instrument to support errors, su- "perstitions and impieties,—and restore christians to "their just and full liberty *of captivating their under-* "*standing to scripture only*." See his *Religion of Pro-* *testants*, p. 152. 4th edit. 1674. There are, never- theless, some who are too assuming; for they require
of

other eating and drinking, which have no other end, than either that of bodily nourishment, of the proposed communicant, that he draw up, or procure the drawing up his EXPERIENCES; which he is to deliver to persons appointed to be *triers* and *judges* of his meetness; a method that encourages the grimace and hypocrisy of profession: whilst it compliments the vanity and pride of such, who must be thus consulted before his admission. But, how contrary is this practice to the apostolical canon? that makes it every man's own province to enter into an examination of himself, and to judge of his own meetness; which, no doubt, is just and reasonable. And assured we are, all other methods are unauthorized, either by by our Lord, or by his apostles. We also here plainly discern, that *infants* are absolutely incapable of the celebration; because they are not of ability for forming any judgment of the design of the Eucharist, or of the requisite self-examination.

And as to all grown persons, who are not in earnest in their religious profession, but remain under the tyranny of some lust or passion, they will not be able *to discern the Lord's body*, or to eat and drink worthily; because the due participation does imply integrity of mind, and an unreservedness in devotion. *We cannot drink the cup of the Lord, and at the same time drink the cup of demons*, 1 Cor. x. 21, which is a contradiction men would gladly reconcile, who partake of the Eucharist, whilst allowing themselves in some criminal gratification.

rifhment, elfe the gratification of the palate or tafte. Whereas this eating and drinking has a fpiritual moral meaning and end; for it is an open focial act, which acknowledges the fpiritual and heavenly benefits of our living upon *his* inftructions, who died without the gates of Jerufalem, a moft fhameful, ignominious, and painful death.

The literal and grofs idea of eating his flefh, and drinking his bloud, could never have entered the heart of man, had not ignorance, fuperftition, and a fondnefs of myftery, fuggefted the extravagance.—When the divine Jefus ufed thofe high figures, *of eating his flefh and drinking his bloud*, he knew the people had been accuftomed to them; for their *lawgiver* had

gratification. Yet no man can duly partake of the Eucharift, who is the flave of fome luft.

But then all his other acts of homage, are likewife fo many expreffions of hypocrify. He will certainly be condemned by the judge, " whofe confcience is not " void of offence, both toward God and toward man." All fuch perfons, therefore, muft be unfit for this holy communion, though of this unfitnefs, they themfelves may be the only competent judges.

informed

informed them, *that man lives not by bread alone, but by every word which proceedeth out of the mouth of God, does man live*, Deut. viii. 3. And besides this, our Lord would not be mistaken by any disciple; for he explains himself in the very same discourse. " It is " the spirit that quickneth, the flesh pro- " fiteth nothing: my words they are spirit, " and they are life," *Joh.* vi. 63. Hence, " his TEACHINGS are that living bread which " came down from heaven; of which, if a " man eat, he shall live for ever." To be able therefore to digest, as well as to taste with pleasure, his instructions, verily is, *to eat his flesh, and drink his blood.* So that all pious persons who discern this doctrine of the Eucharist, are duly qualified for the celebration; they, as the apostle expresseth himself, *can discern his body.* And surely, not any thing is more reasonable, natural, or significant, than this sense of eating the memorial bread, and drinking the memorial cup, as a religious avowal of our devotedness to truth and God, upon the very plan of *his* teachings, whose death we thereby commemorate.

Upon

Upon the whole, it is evident, that an honeſt mind, perſuaded of *Jeſus* being the promiſed Saviour of the world, and that the goſpel hiſtory does contain the ſcheme of his heavenly inſtructions, and who is, at the ſame time, deſirous to approve himſelf a diſciple and ſervant of this one Lord, has an undoubted right, as he is duly qualified for celebrating the Euchariſtical memorials of his ſufferings and death.

§. V. *The chriſtian's obligation to celebrate the Euchariſt, perpetual.*

The perpetuity of the inſtitution, might be argued from its nature, deſign, and tendency.—But let us look back, and a little contemplate the propriety and fitneſs of the celebration, of which notice has been already taken under the firſt ſection. From the face of facts, as they are found in the ſacred records, ſuch celebration was highly reaſonable; inaſmuch as by prophecy and promiſe, *this ſeed of the woman* was ſo conſpicuouſly diſtinguiſhed from all others of mankind; and accordingly, a general expectation of him did

did obtain at the very time of his birth. The Jews were very well affured he muft be one of their own nation, of the feed of *Abraham*, and of the family of *David*. Nor were they lefs confident that when he once came, he would take the fceptre, and affert a civil fovereignty, eftablifhing an univerfal empire! and that under his rule, they fhould be indulged in every fenfitive and animal gratification. No fooner did they find themfelves miftaken in him, whom they would have made their KING, or *captain general*, but they confpired againft him as an impoftor and blafphemer; and put him to a moft ignominious, dolorous, and cruel death.

Thus the facts ftand in the facred record. —And can any human mind think it reafonable, that fuch an event fhould be buried in oblivion? that no monument fhould be erected, that might live throughout the ages of the world, and tranfmit the aftonifhing treatment of this divine character to all nations, as well as to all ages? this will be allowed to be reafonable indeed, if all mankind, of every fucceeding age, are found interefted terested in his ministrations and appointments, whom the great God has constituted *Lord over the dead and the living.*—But this divine intention is fully accomplished by the Eucharist; at the same time it is extremely difficult to conceive of any other possible method of transmitting the evidence so expressively and universally.

The beneficial ends, attainable from the celebration of the Eucharist, by the first christians, are equally yet attainable; and will remain so, whilst the christian is exposed to danger by the impressions of this material system; whilst any trials of his faith and patience remain; or, so long as a finished example of humility, resignation, and fortitude can avail him of benefit, so long the religious celebration of the Eucharist will be found divinely useful to the christian.

But besides the nature and end of the institution, from whence we might argue its *perpetuity*, we have the testimony of an apostle, who assures us, " that he received of
" the

" the Lord, by revelation, that chriſtians do
" celebrate the memorials of his death till
" he come," 1 *Cor.* ii. 26. *As often as ye eat
this bread and drink this cup, ye do ſhew, or
ſhew ye the Lord's death till he come.* It would
be groundleſs to conclude that he meant, *till
the effuſion of the ſpirit*; becauſe this teſtimony concerning the Euchariſt, was given
long after that coming of Chriſt: and the ex-
hortation would therefore have been imper-
tinent. Altogether as unreaſonable it muſt
be to underſtand it, *of his coming to the de-
ſtruction of Jeruſalem*; becauſe the liturgy
of the chriſtian church at Corinth had no
ſort of dependence on the fate of the He-
brew polity, or national ſyſtem. And one
might add the teſtimonies already mentioned
of *Pliny*, *Tatian*, and others, which harmo-
niouſly ſhew, that it has been the univerſal
practice of the chriſtian church to celebrate
the memorials of Chriſt's death, by eating
and drinking euchariſtically.

Farther, there cannot, we preſume, be
one ſingle reaſon adduced, that would ſhew

the obfervance to be of lefs propriety or ufe, though the *coming of Chrift* fhould be applied to the end of the lives of any given number of the firft chriftians; forafmuch as Jefus did exprefsly declare, *that the gates of hades or death fhould not prevail againft his church.* Confequently, what did ferve to diftingifh the firft difciples, by a religious focial tranfaction, in their day, would remain the duty of chriftians in all after-ages; inafmuch as they have ever had but one and the fame invariable and univerfal rule of faith and worfhip. If therefore we fhould apply the coming of Chrift to the ultimate completion of the Catholic church, it will fignify *the end of the world.* And verily, this evidence of the truth of chriftianity exhibited by the Eucharift, will not wax old and infirm, nor diminifh in its vigour, unlefs we can fuppofe that the truth and grace of God may hereafter become of lefs ufe and benefit to mankind: the obligation to obferve the ritual, muft then remain in full force, fo long as it can be profitable to the chriftian to contemplate the cleareft manifeftation of the propitious

nature

nature of God; the freeness of pardoning mercy; and the plenitude of that grace, which has promised eternal life to all who shall be in earnest in the christian profession.

§. VI. *The erroneous and superstitious opinions, which have obtained concerning the Eucharist.*

It is apparent, from St. PAUL's epistle to the *Corinthians*, that christians had, in his day, very much perverted the design of the Eucharist. They did not preserve the religion of the ritual; but they eat and drank to excess.—In very early ages of the church, they had likewise covered the ritual with mystery; and accordingly had their " *Missa Fi-*
" *delium,* or communion service, so called,
" because none might be present at it but
" communicants only, as appears from so-
" lemn forms of dismissing all others before it
" began.*" This was a service distinguished from the *Missa Catechumenorum,* which preceded the prayers at the altar.

* BINGHAM's Ch. Antiq. B. XIII. c. i. sec. 3.

But how high their superstition did run about the Eucharist, may be seen from the custom of giving it to *infants*. " So, in the
" time of *Cyprian*, it was usual for children
" and sucking infants to receive the sacra-
" ment, unto whom it was necessary parti-
" cularly to deliver the elements.—And
" when a sucking girl refused to taste the sa-
" cramental wine, the deacon violently
" forced it down her throat.*" The other hiftorian says, " it was a known practice and
" custom in the ancient church, of giving
" the Eucharist to *infants*, which continued
" in the church for several ages. It is fre-
" quently mentioned in *Cyprian*, *Austin*,
" *Innocentius* and *Gennadius*, writers from
" the third to the fifth century. *Maldonat*
" confesses it was in the church for six hun-
" dred years.†" And *again*, " it is beyond
" dispute that the church baptized infants,
" and gave them the unction of chrism
" with imposition of hands for confirma-
" mation, so she immediately admitted them

* L. King's constitutions, &c. Part II. ch. vi. sec. 6.
† Bingham's Ch. Antiq. B. XII. ch. i. sec. 3.

"to a participation of the Eucharift, as
"foon as they were baptized, and ever after
"without exception.*"

Nay, Dr. WHITBY has obferved, that Mr. DALLY, in a large chapter on that fubject (referring us to his *De cultibus*) has proved, "that it was the conftant cuftom of
"the whole church of God, from the *third*
"to the *twelfth* century, to minifter the Eu-
"charift to baptized infants; which thing
"they alfo declared to be *neceffary* for the
"remiffion of fins, and the falvation of the
"infant; and alfo pleaded fcripture for the
"proof of what they faid." See his *prot. recon.* p. 289, 290. An idea of the *church*, not much to its reputation, and would lead us to conclude, that ignorance and fuperftition were its chief pillars.

To fuch an aftonifhing height of extravagance, *ecclefiaftics* were wont to carry their fuperftitious regards to the Eucharift. They

* BINGHAM's Antiq. B. XV. c. iv. fec. 7.

had

had first affixed to BAPTISM a regenerating efficacy; and when they had once done this, they could apply to the baptized whatever they fancied did, or might possibly belong to the christian system of ritual.* In this superstitious

* It is of the nature of enthusiasm, to run all its "opinions into extremes:" else one would be astonished at finding any ascribe to baptism, an *instantaneous* regenerating power. For verily, we can be very confident, that the *New Testament* never once inculcates on the mind of the reader such an idea of baptism. On the contrary, it always supposes, that those *adult* persons whe desired baptism, were already become believers; and not that baptism had had the converting and regenerating effect. Baptism, verily, did no more to them than it did to their infants, *i. e.* it iniated both the one and the other into a kingdom or constitution of truth and mercy; and entitled them to the immunities and privileges of a divine polity. Yet some who would be called Protestants, have said as extravagant things of *baptism*, as " Pagans in *India* do of the purifying virtue
" of the river *Ganges*, to which they ascribe a saving
" influence: for however immoral their lives, if they
" are but plunged in the river *Ganges*, they shall find
" their way, without any difficulty, to the regions of
" light and happiness."—*Writers*, who consult the sense of the church, rather than that of the sacred cannon, may be expected to deliver very crude and absurd
notions

stitious application of an heavenly divine ritual, we may well conclude, that the church would be disposing apace for a farther degeneracy: and anon we read of oecumenical councils *transubstantiating* the elements of bread and wine, used at the memorial supper, into the real body and blood of Christ. And upon no better foundation than that of Christ's saying, *this is my body*. It is therefore ordained, that men believe the real presence of Christ, when the priest has once consecrated the elements. The communicant is taught to imagine, that when Jesus brake the bread, he brake his own body; and when he bade them *take and eat*, he bade them *take and eat* his own body; that when each of his disciples had eaten an whole body, he arose from table and went out with them, his body being unbroken and uneaten; and in that condition was ap-

notions about *faith*, *grace*, *baptism*, and *regeneration*. But so it has been, we see, in those ages of the church, when not content with baptizing infants, they must apply to them not only the useless, frivolous, paultry rites of *chrism* and *confirmation*, but even the divine rite of the Eucharist.

I prehended,

prehended, after he had agonized in the garden.

Nay, there is an addition made to this extravagance, for what is called the Romish apostolic church has mutilated or maimed the plan of celebration: inasmuch as because Jesus has expresly said of the cup, *drink ye all of it;* the presuming priest only drinks of the cup, and will not suffer the laity a taste with him. So studious has *popery* been, in all possible ways, to prevert the original plain design of this divine institution.

Other churches there are, who reject *transubstantiation*, or deny a change of the elements into the real body and bloud of Christ; which yet hold a substantial presence of Christ with the elements.—The opinion of the *Greek* church; the *Lutheran* tenet of consubstantiation, or impanation.

A more modern monstrous perversion of the Eucharist, is that of making a celebration thereof, the communicant's necessary qualification for civil honours and worldly profits.

profits. A ritual, that was defigned to fet before all chriftians the exemplary contempt which our bleffed Lord had of the world, is thus made the requifite means of gratifying avarice and ambition, in the communicant. —What?—could no greater fecurity be given of loyalty to a prince, or of fidelity to a civil conftitution, than to celebrate the memorials of *his* death who refufed the civil preferment, and rejected with difdain the fecular honour! the abfurdity is fo glaring, that we cannot forbear making this conclufion, *viz.* that becaufe one fort of nominal chriftians had been capable of inventing or creating that monfter, TRANSUBSTANTIATION! another fort would try if they could not match the invention, with an equally fhocking abfurdity! but, what child is there who cannot fee the unreafonablenefs of fuppofing, fuch a flagrant proftitution of a divine appointment (by the one heavenly Lord) a good fecurity of allegiance to an earthly prince, and of the reverence due to the majefty of a free people?

It deserves seriously to be considered, by all who revere this holy rite, whether such celebration be not to eat this bread, and drink this cup of the Lord *unworthily?* i. e. even so as to be guilty of *prophaning* the symbols of the body and bloud of the Lord. They who partake of the Eucharist without any meaning, or with one quite foreign to the design of the institution, do, in the sense of an apostle, incur *judgment* on themselves, not discerning the Lord's body. On which account, he tells us, many Corinthian christians *were sickly, and many slept*. The hand of God did punish such wanton acts of impiety in the first christians, in order to inspire with caution the after-communicant, and create a becoming veneration of the ritual. It was in demonstration of its divine original, and pointed out the necessity there was of examining and judging of themselves, that they might not be judged and condemned with the world.

Many of the churches abovementioned, have made use of the Eucharist as a *charm*,
expecting

expecting it to operate even in the dying hour; and by a kind of forcery, they thereon give abfolution, and declare it a good PASSPORT to heaven. Here will be requifite, a blind implicit faith in the receiver; and no fmall affurance in the adminiftrator.

QUAKERISM, by avoiding all thefe extremes, has apparently run into another; and inftead of celebrating thefe memorials of the fufferings and death of Chrift, has reprefented the obfervance to be only fpiritual and internal. BARCLAY afks, " doth not
" this contending for the ufe of *water,*
" *bread and wine,* as neceffary parts of gof-
" pel worfhip, deftroy the nature of it, as if
" the gofpel were a difpenfation of *fhadows,*
" and not of the *fubftance?*"—He again afks, " what ground from fcripture or rea-
" fon can our adverfaries bring us to evince,
" that one *fhadow* or *figure* fhould point to
" another *fhadow* or *figure,* and not to the
" *fubftance?*" After this he takes notice
" of the fupper having been given to young
" boys and little children: and then ob-
" ferves, what little weight fhould be laid
" upon

" upon antiquity."—See his XIIIth proposition, sections 9th and 10th.

But how very sophistical and delusive this sort of reasoning? it does not, in the least, affect the view we have taken of the doctrine of the Eucharist. Since eating memorial bread, and drinking memorial wine, are, truly and properly, *the monument of a fact*; and not one shadow or figure of another shadow or figure. Even this very *writer*, speaking of the life, death, sufferings and obedience of Christ, says, " they made a " way for our *reconciliation*, and became a " sacrifice for the remission of sins that are " past."—See under his VIIth proposition, p. 226. By his own confession therefore, the sufferings and death, and obedience of Christ, which we recognize in the *Eucharist*, are facts, yea, they are with him interesting facts; and therefore cannot but deserve a religious commemoration. Yet it must be confessed, that in very modern times, and in more reformed churches, much *superstition* has prevailed about the Eucharist.

Of the doctrine of the Eucharist.

Eucharist. In some, a solemnity is given to it, by the *infrequency* of the celebration. The communion tables are crowded, where it is administred but annually, or at best quarterly; with preparation days, to create the greater reverence. In others, *Christmas Day* and *Good Friday* have an emphasis laid upon them; though the *New Testament* canon never mentions the christians breaking memorial bread, on any other than the *first* day of the week.* And, in truth, such is the superstitious disposition of the professing christian world, that the more any ritual is covered with *mystery*, and made important by bigo-

* Some difficulty seems to arise in the way of the *Sabbatarian*, who will sanctify the *seventh*, and not the the *first* day of the week; *i. e.* if the breaking of bread on the first day, mentioned by LUKE, intends the Eucharist, (as we have understood it to be a distinguishing ritual in the christian liturgy) then the practice of the *Sabbatarian* is not so defensible. We also lay stress on the christian's making charitable collections on that day, 1 *Cor.* xvi. 2. and on *John*'s mentioning the *Lord's Day*, *Apoc.* i. 10. And if the pentecost effusion of the spirit was also on that day, it must be held distinguishingly sacred, in the esteem of christians.—See and consult LIGHTFOOT's works, vol. II. p. 642.

try,

try, the more numerous and devout are its obfervers.

§. VII. *Obfervations made on the doctrine.*

1. It was certainly known to be an undeniable fact, in the firft age of the obfervance, that the Eucharift was inftituted by Jefus Chrift himfelf, juft as the gofpel hiftory reports; elfe it could never have become the *diftinguifhing* ritual of chriftian focial worfhip. We are affured, it could not be of *later* original, than the *New Teftament* report has made of it: for had it not at firft been well attefted by a fufficient number of credible witneffes, tradition would have been too flender a fupport for this kind of celebration. Nay, had it not been the diftinguifhing ritual of the firft chriftians focial worfhip, it could never have obtained fuch obfervance; becaufe in the whole facred hiftory of the ritual, as it lies in the canon, it is fo reprefented. But if there had been any fallacy in this report, made by the apoftle *Paul* and the evangelift *Luke*, when writing the hiftory of the firft planting of
the

the chriftian church, the attempt to recommend and enforce fuch a *fingular* obfervance, muft have been treated with deferved ridicule and contempt.

Nor have we the leaft reafon to fuppofe, that fuch an inftitution would have been inferted by three of the four evangelifts, or *biographers*, who drew up the life of Chrift, had they not feen, that the inftitution itfelf was worthy of him; and muft be an immortal monument of a fact, which is univerfally and everlaftingly interefting to mankind.

Indeed in the firft celebration, as performed by Chrift and his apoftles, it could not be called the *memorial* of a fact which was yet future; but then that very ritual fo inftituted, was in all after-times to be celebrated as a monument or memorial of *his* fufferings and death, who could, with his difciples, compofedly eat bread and drink wine with *thankfgivings* to God, over thofe views which he had of his own approaching crucifixion.

Our faith may then be firmly established in the *credibility* of the gospel history; since not only the nature, design, and end of the Eucharist, but the circumstances of its origination, render it utterly improbable, if not absolutely impossible, that it should have owed its existence to any artful contrivance, or political invention. Nay, we might infer its genuinely divine original, from the various amazing superstitions which have obtained, in the celebration of it among christians.

II. The plainness, purity, and moral tendency of the institution, should recommend the Eucharist to the celebration of all sincere believers. The expressive simplicity of it is manifest; being no other than to eat bread and drink wine (those natural supports and cordials of animal human life) in commemoration of *his* sufferings and death, who has shewn us, by his instructions, what are the real and true principles of spiritual and immortal life: since by his crucifixion we we are taught, what must be the deadly tendency

dency of all those propensities and indulgences, which are of a groveling and worldly complexion. We see how *the iniquities of men*, governed by lust, *did meet upon him*. And in what a convincing manner he has exposed to our aversion and abhorrence, all *that is of the world*.

Again, the very celebration has an heavenly and divine tendency; since we openly, solemnly profess, by that transaction, to approve his conduct, to admire and emulate the greatness of his mind, who, when he was led to *Calvary*, moved meekly along, *just as a lamb goes to the slaughter, and as a sheep before her devourers is dumb, so he opened not his mouth*. By this commemoration, we avow a resolution to resemble him in temper and life; keeping ourselves free from all tyrannizing and enslaving passions; such as avarice, pride and sensuality. We gain a farther advantage, by contemplating him, as sustaining the torture with so much dignity, from *the eye he had to the recompence of reward*. With such reference we also become enabled to support under every present painful endurance.

Moreover, because he has assured us, that he went to the heavenly house of his father, with designs of preparing mansions for our everlasting happy enjoyment; nay, even to take us to himself to behold the glory which the father hath given him, in order to our confirmation and establishment in holiness: we, at his table, ruminate on the promise; solace ourselves in the prospect; quicken and invigorate all our preparations for his pleasing and transporting advent.

These are plain, rational, expressive doctrines of the *Eucharist*, which should persuade every sincere christian to a very devout observance.—And surely no one who believes that Christ spake, with an intention to be obeyed by all his followers, when he said, DO THIS IN REMEMBRANCE OF ME, can have a reasonable objection: because it obliges him to no more duties and services, than he is already willing, nay, desirous to perform.—The sincere christian cannot think that his Lord would have appointed this memorial, had he not seen the reasonableness and usefulness of it: forasmuch as he will readily

readily allow that his divine master had wisdom given him *equal* to his mission, character, and appointments.

More may be said for the omission of those christians, who have been discouraged from misrepresentation and misapprehension; awed by a wrong education, and deep-rooted prejudices. Yet even those professors should honestly endeavour to remove prejudice, and understand clearly the nature and design of this institution. They should; for there is something very unaccountable in their conduct, who can satisfy themselves in a course of life, of which they hope neither to be afraid or ashamed, when they come into the presence of the judge; who are, nevertheless, either afraid or ashamed of coming to his table. Unaccountable indeed it must be, that a man shall not think himself fitly qualified for commemorating Christ's death, who has no kind of uneasiness about his meetness for the judicial presence of Christ.

Does he say, *truly it is very unfashionable; and he chuseth not to have the sneer and ridicule of his acquaintance and companions!*
Such

Such a one would do well to consider, and ask himself, whether the good opinion of Christ, or of his companions, will promise him the most satisfaction?—There is great and weighty meaning in that declaration of our Lord's.—*Whosoever shall confess me before men, him will I confess also before my father which is in heaven. But whosoever shall deny me before men, him will I also deny before my father who is in heaven.* May it not be applicable to this, as well as to any other kind of confession? How far it is, every one should judge impartially for himself.

III. Some well-meaning christians are deterred and affrighted from the table of the Lord, principally because St. PAUL speaks of the unworthy communicant's eating and drinking *damnation*, or *judgment* to himself; when it is evident, that the *Corinthians* did very prophanely pervert the design of the Eucharist. They were intemperate in the festival; they eat and drank to excess; and the rich separated themselves from the poor, allowing them no fellowship with them. Which the apostle reproves, by saying, " my bre-
" thren,

"thren, when ye come together to eat, *i. e.* the Eucharist, tarry one for another. But if any man hunger, let him eat at home; that ye come not together unto *condemnation.*"—There is therefore no reason of dread or terror, to any serious and conscientious christian, in his approach to the table of the Lord, because of these declarations about eating and drinking unworthily, thereby incurring damnation or judgment. But every man may be assured of escaping such censure, who eats and drinks in acknowledgment of his devotedness to the one Lord, whose advent he is daily waiting for.

F I N I S.

BOOKS printed for C. HENDERSON.

A Survey of a search after Souls, 8vo, 4s.
No Protestant Popery, a Sermon, 6d.
Recovery from Sickness, 3d.

Where may be had, just published,
The Palladium of Great Britain and Ireland, 2s. 6d.

www.ingramcontent.com/pod-product-compliance
Lightning Source LLC
Chambersburg PA
CBHW020338090426
42735CB00009B/1584